W9-BIM-117

For the boys and girls
of the E.M. Baker School
— M.B.

Special thanks to Laurie Roulston
of the Denver Museum of Natural History
for her expertise

Photography credits:

Cover and page 3: James D. Watt/Innerspace Visions; pages 1 and 13: Bill Curtsinger; page 4: Ben Cropp/Innerspace Visions; page 5: Norbert Wu; page 6: Chris A. Crumley/EarthWater Stock Photography; page 7: Bill Curtsinger; pages 8-9: Mark Conlin/Innerspace Visions; page 10: Ron & Valerie Taylor/Innerspace Visions; page 11: Walt Stearns/Innerspace Visions; page 12: Norbert Wu/Peter Arnold, Inc.; page 14: Doug Perrine and Jose Castro/Innerspace Visions; page 15: Bill Curtsinger; page 17: Michael S. Nolan/Innerspace Visions; page 18: Michel Jozon/Innerspace Visions; page 19: Doug Perrine/Innerspace Visions; page 20: Mark Strickland/Innerspace Visions; pages 21-23: Jeff Rotman; page 24: Fred McConnaughey/Photo Researchers; page 25: Mark Strickland/Innerspace Visions; page 26: Doug Perrine/Innerspace Visions; page 27: Mark Conlin/Innerspace Visions; page 28: Massimo & Lucia Simion/Jeff Rotman; page 29: Jeff Rotman; page 30: Jeff Rotman/Innerspace Visions; page 31: David B. Fleetham/Innerspace Visions; page 32: Doug Perrine/Innerspace Visions; page 33: Bill Curtsinger; page 34: J. Dan Wright/EarthWater Stock Photography; page 35 top and bottom: Norbert Wu; page 36: Douglas Seifert/EarthWater Stock Photography; page 37: Bob Cranston/Innerspace Visions; page 38: Nigel Marsh/ Innerspace Visions; page 39: Mark Conlin/Innerspace Visions; page 40: Kelvin Aitken/Peter Arnold, Inc.

Text copyright © 1999 by Melvin Berger.
All rights reserved. Published by Scholastic Inc.
Printed in the U.S.A.

ISBN 0-439-69328-4

SCHOLASTIC and associated logos and designs are
trademarks and/or registered trademarks of Scholastic Inc.

11 12 13 14 15 16 17 18 19 20   40   14 13

CHOMP!
A Book About Sharks

by Melvin Berger

Scholastic Reader

SCHOLASTIC INC.
New York   Toronto   London   Auckland   Sydney
Mexico City   New Delhi   Hong Kong   Buenos Aires

CHAPTER ONE

Great Hunters

Sharks are fish.

Most are very large.

They have huge appetites.

And they're almost always hunting for

something to eat.

This hungry shark is swimming slowly
back and forth.
Its senses are wide awake.

Suddenly the shark smells something.
It is blood in the water.
The blood is about a mile away.
That's as long as 20 blocks.
The shark speeds toward the smell.

The shark also picks up some faraway
sounds.
The shark's ears are two small holes
in the skin.
It hears something moving in the water.
The shark swims even faster.

The water is dark.

But the shark sees well in little light.

It spots an injured seal.

The seal has been badly cut.

There is blood in the water.

The shark circles around.

It comes in closer and closer.

Suddenly the shark lunges.
CHOMP!
It sinks its teeth into the seal.

The shark rips off a large chunk
of flesh.
GULP!
The shark swallows it whole.

All at once, other sharks appear.
They churn and shake the water.
Each wants the same seal.

The sharks snap and rip at the seal.
They bite each other.
Sometimes they even bite themselves!
It's called a "feeding frenzy."

Soon there is little left of the seal.
The feeding frenzy is over.
The sharks glide away.

Most sharks hunt fish, seals, and porpoises.
But some eat dead or dying animals and shellfish.
A few kinds of sharks feed on tiny sea plants and animals.

CHAPTER TWO

Powerful Swimmers

Sharks seem made for swimming.
Most have sleek, rounded bodies.
They slip easily through the water.

Sharks use their fins to swim.
The big tail fin swings from side to side.
The tail pushes against the water.
It moves the shark forward.
The other fins keep the shark steady
in the water.

Sharks do not have smooth scales like most fish.

Instead they have many sharp, pointed scales.

The points face back toward the tail.

They help water flow over the shark's body — without slowing it down.

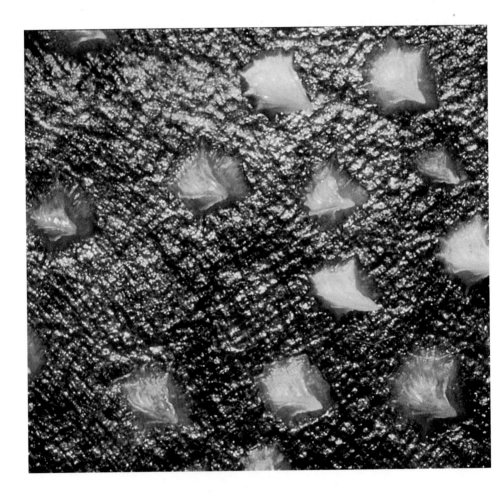

Sharks usually swim about three miles
per hour.
But they can put on bursts of speed.
When hunting, some reach 40 miles
per hour!

Did you know that most sharks swim
all the time?
They swim day and night.
They even swim when asleep!

Swimming and breathing go together.
If sharks stop swimming, they stop
breathing.
And they die.

Sharks breathe oxygen (say "OCK-suh-jun").
We breathe oxygen, too.
Our oxygen comes from the air.
Sharks get their oxygen from the water.

Most sharks swim with open mouths.
Water enters.
It flows over their gills.
The gills take the oxygen from the water.
Then the water flows out.

Swimming also keeps sharks afloat.
If they stop swimming, they sink to
the bottom.

A shark twists and turns as it swims.
That's because it doesn't have a bone
in its body!
A shark's skeleton is made of cartilage
(say "CAR-ti-luj").
And cartilage bends easily.

Your nose has cartilage.
See how easily you can twist and
turn it.

Sharks often swim with two types of trusty friends.

One is the pilot fish.

Pilot fish seem to lead the sharks.

But all they do is catch food that the sharks drop.

The other friend is the remora.
Remoras hitch rides on sharks.
They also eat shellfish that dig into the
sharks' skin.
No wonder sharks don't seem to mind
remoras tagging along.

CHAPTER THREE

Hundreds of Teeth

Sharks have lots of teeth.

Some have hundreds.

A few have thousands.

Imagine brushing that many teeth!

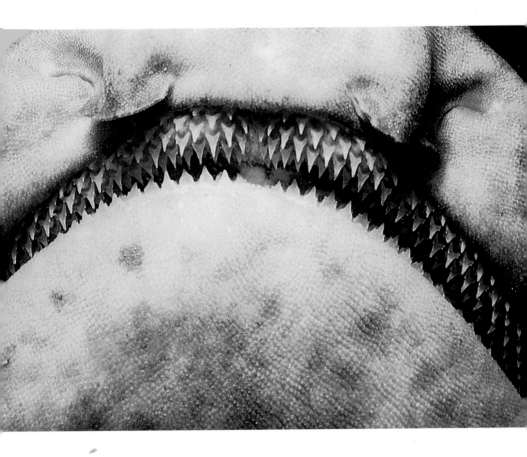

Shark teeth are not in one row like yours.
Sharks have as many as 20 rows
of teeth.
The rows are behind each other.

When a shark is ready to eat, it lifts
its snout.
This pushes the shark's mouth out
in front.
It also bares its teeth.

Sharks have teeth that are fit for what they eat.

- Curved teeth are for biting.
- Pointed teeth are for catching small fish.
- Flat teeth are for crushing shellfish.

Shark teeth do not have roots like yours.
Their teeth often break or fall out.
Then new teeth move up from the
row behind.
They take the place of the lost teeth.

Sharks can lose thousands of teeth in
a lifetime.
Divers find many on the ocean floor.
Sailors used to shave with them!

CHAPTER FOUR

Fantastic Babies

Shark babies are called pups.
Shark mothers usually give birth to a
few pups at a time.

All pups grow from eggs.
In most sharks, the eggs grow inside
the mother.
They can grow there for nearly a year.

When ready, the pups come out of the
mother's body.
But they're not like human babies.
Pups take care of themselves from
the start.
Off they go, to begin the hunt for food.

Some mother sharks lay eggs outside
their bodies.
The eggs are in cases.
The cases fall to the bottom of the sea.

The pup grows inside the egg case.
When it hatches, the pup swims out —
and away!

Sometimes egg cases wash ashore.
People find them on the beach.
They call the cases "mermaids' purses."

CHAPTER FIVE

Curious Creatures

Sharks live all over the world.

- They live in deep water and shallow water.
- They live in cold water and warm water.
- Some even live in rivers and lakes.

Nearly everyone is afraid of sharks.
Yet most rarely harm us.

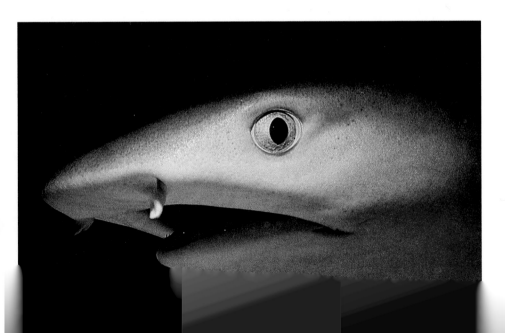

The **great white shark** swims mainly
in deep, cold seas.
Its underside is white.
But its back is dark.
This makes the great white hard to see.
- From below, the shark looks like
  the sky.
- From above, the shark looks like
  the water.

Large animals, such as sea lions, fall
prey to the great white shark.

The **bull shark** is mostly found in
shallow water.
Sometimes it swims into rivers
or lakes.
A short snout and stout body make it
look like a bull.
That's how it got its name.

The **blue shark** is easy to spot.
It lives in the deepest part of the
ocean.
Yet it swims near the surface.
Its fins stick up out of the water.
Blues often swim together in
large groups.

Some people call the **tiger shark**
a "swimming garbage can."
It will eat just about anything.
A fisherman once caught a tiger shark.
In its belly he found

- nine shoes,
- a belt,
- and a pair of pants!

One of the smallest sharks is the
dwarf shark.

It is only about six inches long.

You could hold one in your hand.

The biggest shark is the **whale shark**.
It can be as long and heavy as a
tractor trailer!
Sometimes the whale shark stands
upright in the water.
It bobs up and down, swallowing whole
schools of small fish.

The **hammerhead shark** looks odd,
to say the least.
It has a thick bar across the front of
its head.
And its eyes are at the ends of the bar.
No one is sure why.

It's easy to mistake the **carpet shark** for a rug.

It lays still on the ocean bottom.

Fringes around its snout make it look messy.

But let a fish swim by.

The carpet shark whips around and grabs it!

The **angel shark** is no angel.

It hides in reefs or caves under the
water.

Or it digs its body into the sand.

Nearby shellfish have to be careful.

The angel shark is always ready
to pounce.

Now you know.

Sharks

- are mighty hunters,
- are powerful swimmers,
- have lots of teeth,
- give birth to pups,
- live almost everywhere,
- and come in all sizes and shapes.

They're really amazing!